Attention Large Hairless Subordinate

20 emails from my cat that made me a better leader.

Reflections on Leadership

By Timothy Hagler

"I want to be the person my dog thinks I am." A meaningful reflection for certain, but I really don't know who to attribute it to… Do you? Can you tell me? If so please do! Various permutations of this saying have attained memetic ubiquity status as internet quips, t-shirt graphics, and books of all sorts. I have heard it prayed; "Dear Lord, help me to be the person my dog thinks I am", and I have seen it on resumes; "My personal objective is to be the person… and so on" I first heard it from an old boss of mine who offered it at the start of a divisional meeting as a centering reflection.

For as much depth as the statement has, it started me wondering "since I live in a dog-free family, just who does my CAT think I am? More importantly, do I live up to her expectation?"

Animal behaviorists have long told us that dogs don't think we are other dogs. Dogs play and interact with other dogs differently than they play and relate to humans. Cats, on the other hand; do not display distinguishable behavioral differences as they engage with humans or other cats. They evidently see us as just other feline acquaintance, and as such, the race is on for household dominance.

You know that dogs like you if both of you are breathing. Even fierce dogs are most likely displaying behavior that was "taught" to them in some way by a human.

Cats have a long list of "I guess you are OK" cues to demonstrate their tribal acceptance. The tail rub, resting in contact with you, purring, mutual grooming, and slow blinking are all part of their 'tolerate and cohabitate' ritual.

Back to the seminal question, "what kind of person does my cat think I am?" In my careful (non-scientific) study, conducted over several cups of morning coffee, I am convinced that to Sabel (my cat), I am a 'large hairless subordinate.' Oh, she is very loving and thrives on affection from the entire family, but as I have come to realize, this affection is simply our job and we are required to deliver it in a specific manner at specific times. If we enjoy our subordinate affection duties and responsibilities, well, that is just icing on our cake. Consider that a 'perquisite.'

One morning while nursing the first cup of Joe for the day, and taking care of a few early emails, I began to ponder how my perceived role in a cat-led household reflects on developing and augmenting actual human leadership qualities and traits. "I wonder what an email from Sabel would be like? What would she write to her 'large hairless subordinate'? How would she provide the influence and inspiration that are the trademarks of leadership in this electronic communication forum?" After all, email is perfect for a cat! Void of emotional connection yet likely to have the reader attribute emotion to it, aloof but not withdrawn enough to be squarely disengaged, and certainly effective at shunting the monkey from the sender's back to that of the receiver without warning — but memorialized in writing and now undeniable and irrefutable. I thought it was time to put some cat email down on paper and see what lessons can be learned.

Here are 20 such "inspirational" emails from Sabel.

Also to my wife Kandy, who has time after time been awarded "subordinate of the month" by Sabel. Kandy is my coach, best friend, and favorite non-cat life form of all time. And to all the sporting goods distributors who have sold us a mountain of ping pong balls (Sabel's only officially approved toy) over the years. I would as well like to dedicate this book to my mentors, and those who have blessed me by challenging me to awaken great leadership talent in them.

SABEL THE CAT

Contents

From:	SabelTheCat
Sent:	Monday 2:03 AM
To:	Tim
Subject:	You need a back-up

Attn. Large Hairless Subordinate:

It occurs to me that you are packing the black rolling box you drag behind you when you leave... In fact, you are often away from home for days on end, and I wait here with the smaller, high-performing subordinate. While she is better at her affection and grooming duties, you respond much more generously to my commands at feeding time. Please train the high-performing subordinate as your food service back-up. While we are on the subject, you are gone a lot. It wouldn't hurt to always be training an intern.

STC

As a leader you need to face the reality that for as hard as it is to think of right now, you will not always be the leader for the team you have now. There will always be disruption; management restructures, mergers, health issues, new opportunities, and new callings in life that will take you in new and interesting directions. This is a healthy condition. A normal condition of the workplace. Just look at the wall in the office with all the portraits of leaders who came before you, one or two of them are probably people you look up to, someone who blazed the trail for you in distinct and tactile ways.

This is also why Sabel has a point that we need to always allow for talent stewardship capacity on our teams. We should always have an "intern" as Sabel puts it in her 2AM email. Robert Frost claimed that the 'secret sauce' of a mentor and teacher was to actually be "an awakener." Awakening the great leadership talent on your team will extend YOUR influence and leadership for generations beyond your service as future leaders talk about your pioneering influence while they point out your portrait on the wall to their apprentice.

From:	SabelTheCat
Sent:	Thursday 1:23 PM
To:	Tim
Subject:	What is your "thing" anyway?

Attn. Large Hairless Subordinate:

It has come to my attention, that I have no idea just what you are about. I am concerned that you don't know either. You are good at food service in terms of quantity, but not so good at affection, and you groom "every now and then." And you waste prime napping-in-the-sun-time staring at the bright picture box. When you are not just staring at it, you are yelling at it... "Run a twin tight end and hit the weak side, you know - where the nickel ain't! Who thought you to call a play?" What does that even mean? Again - Just what is your "thing" anyway?

STC

It is easy to explain our leadership "thing" in terms of being ROAD WORTHY. It's an acronymous pneumonic device for R-O-A-D-(*D*).

Build great RELATIONSHIPS. Leadership is a people business.

Take OWNERSHIP for everything you have influence over, especially when that influence benefits your team.

Be ACCOUNTABLE for all those things that are the direct work of your team and your discipline. Budgets, revenues, productivity, plans, deadlines, and process improvements.

And at all times, demonstrate DEPENDABILITY.

When all that is accomplished you will have earned the requisite respect to be able to deliver DECISIVENESS (yes, I cheated by adding a second "D") when command moments arise. And remember when those decisive moments do come your way, be an effective commander when necessary, but return the team to normal operations roles and norms as soon as possible. In business, command is a moment of necessary decisiveness, not a permanent condition.

From:	SabelTheCat
Sent:	Wednesday 2:52 AM
To:	Tim
Subject:	Sharing Treats

Attn. Large Hairless Subordinate:

I would like to bring it to your attention that when you go to the bottom left cupboard door to get a crunchy snack for you, it would be good form to bring me a handful of crunchy treats as well. If I can figure out how to get in there and open the bag, I would spread some potato chips out on the floor for both of us. I think you should do the same. Sharing is a recommended practice. It's something for you to work on.

STC

Sabel has a point... Our accomplishment and success can have a positive effect on many people.

Dedicate yourself fully to the things that give your life significance and purpose.

Better yourself.

Don't be shy.

Connect.

Share what you know.

Be authentic.

Get to the root of the issue.

Invest in others.

Influence.

If someone is treated unfairly, take up their fight.

Allow your tide to rise... All boats will lift with you!

From:	SabelTheCat
Sent:	Sunday 3:00 PM
To:	Tim
Subject:	Stop doing stupid stuff

Attn. Large Hairless Subordinate:

I have noticed that instead of attending to your feline food service duties, lately you have been preoccupied with stupid stuff that shows up on the bright picture box. You are now yelling at moving pictures of men throwing a giant orange cat toy into a suspended basket of some kind. Get real. Focus on your duties and stop doing stupid stuff.

STC

One of my old bosses once told me "Leaders of all disciplines just need to stop doing stupid stuff! If we all stop doing stupid stuff, the remainder will be all the excellent stuff."

What a powerful and simple message. Every 'stupid' thing we stop doing increases our effectiveness in multiple dimensions! What a great investment of time, to just reflect and discern for a moment on what we do as leaders that is just plain stupid and then set out to immediately curtail that behavior! Here is a list to get started.

Stupid Thing #1

Taking all the credit for the project or an employee's idea or plan.

Stupid Thing #2

Letting the wrong people take up too much of our time. This exhibits itself in:

Making rules to control the actions of a few employees that must be extended to the many.

Keeping the wrong people – for too long.

Listening and responding to complainers first.

Stupid Thing #3

Failing to think beyond our own little world and thus, neglecting to communicate the most important information to employees and stakeholders.

Stupid Thing #4

Being wimpy. The "wimp" often shows up when –

Exhibiting a lack of decisiveness.

Being too inclusive just to placate the wrong people.

Stupid Thing #5

Not taking the time to craft compelling, reason- and-data-driven business case to support the great work of our teams and critical collaborators.

Friends, how wonderful it feels to get the stupid stuff off the agenda, and to know that we are clear to pursue the excellent work we are driven to accomplish.

From: SabelTheCat
Sent: 3:45 PM
To: Tim
Subject: Lacking Energy

Attn. Large Hairless Subordinate:

I lack the energy to climb steps in the early morning hours. From now on I am implementing a policy of caterwauling at the foot of the stairs at 1 or 2 in the morning to be carried upstairs to continue morning napping. Please be prompt but if you aren't don't worry I will gradually increase volume and intensity of my yodeling for your convenience.

STC

To Demonstrate:

> Passion
> Enthusiasm
> Vivid communication
> Robust laughter
> Healthy, happy appearance
> Highly motivational leadership

You need:

> A good night's sleep
> Exercise (regular, not necessarily strenuous)

A solid diet, healthy food, portion control, eat for the effect it will have on your energy level

Avoidance of energy draining, negative people, and situations

To read positive (educational, motivational) material

Inspiration - look for it everywhere

Opportunity

The decision and the commitment to be energetic!

From:	SabelTheCat
Sent:	4:38 PM
To:	Tim
Subject:	Jealous Much?

Attn. Large Hairless Subordinate:

You threw me off mama's lap... Just so you could get your ugly hairless feet rubbed. Jealousy is soooo ugly on you. It's something to work on. And get me a kibble.

STC

New processes, bringing in new colleagues, starting up new business or service lines, investing in new ventures, new digital systems, finding new markets, assessing new opportunities, M&A, planned disruptions, value engineering...

What if the FIRST-BEST hurdle rate was not ROI or NPV, but it was "how does this [new] campaign demonstrate support for the success of the highly organizationally-aligned initiatives and efforts of peers and colleagues? What if my initiative was allowed to shine basking in the bright light of 100 suns, rather than the forced illumination of my own dim bulb?

We are often so concerned about competing with the potential of colliding initiatives or campaigns that rob the organizational will and attention from our team's strategic effort, that we forget that there is a value in contributing to the progressive momentum of our colleague's success.

As Sabel always tells me… "It's something to work on." (Cats have notoriously poor grammar.)

From:	SabelTheCat
Sent:	6:30 PM
To:	Tim
Subject:	Scaredy Cat!

Attn. Large Hairless Subordinate:

Honestly, the neighbor's snarling Rottweiler frightens you? Just hiss at it and give it a quick 15 swipes with your claws out then get over it!

STC

Sabel had it partly right... For her, it isn't about the size of the cat in the fight, but the size of the fight in the cat that determines whether fear is justified or not.

Robert Kennedy said it this way - "Only those who dare to fail greatly can ever achieve greatly." Great leaders know that failure and success are two horns on the same goat.

When facing a tough situation where fearful leaders would melt away into rationalizing the situation into a perceived low-risk version of being "safely but directionally correct"... STOP – and:

Face the truth:

> Reality check – yourself – have a cohort that will help you see past your desire to "normalize" the story.
>
> What does the "data" show?
>
> What are you going to do about it now that you are facing it head-on?

Ship it:

> Be decisive, have a bias for action.
>
> Launch.
>
> Study, but be a quick study, decide quickly, act quickly.
>
> Adjust course in flight.
>
> Stop getting ready to get ready already.

Accept responsibility freely when something goes wrong.

> Stop the blame game in its tracks.
>
> You have permission to grow and develop when you take responsibility.
>
> You own the fix.
>
> You retain driving the results.
>
> Move on... Failures and mistakes can't keep you from achieving your goals.

But most of all fight the paralysis of being afraid that you may not actually be fearless. Just start by knowing that most of the time fear of failure is a natural emotion when you are pushing the envelope. Look around, you are not alone – ask for help from other leaders when you are fearful, just remember to reciprocate when colleagues need a stronger confidant to stand steadfast with them in their uncertain times. Think through the worst case scenario... Now that you know what that is it will be manageable... Let replace the "worst case" with "plan B" and acknowledge that plan B doesn't make you a failure... It just means you pick up the pieces and course-correct.

From:	SabelTheCat
Sent:	12:05 AM
To:	Tim
Subject:	Day Dreaming (about better kibble)

Attn. Large Hairless Subordinate:

I wonder how glorious my free-feeding experience would be if you could put just a fraction of the attention in preparing my kibble that you put in those Dagwood hoagie creations that you tempt your arteries' fate with at 11:00 at night? Oh well, a cat can have daydreams.

STC

In South Carolina, we are fanatical about NASCAR racing... We live the fantasy on the freeways as well, and it makes driving the shopping mall a high-acuity event! It's not really a need for speed, but rather just a need to be in the lead. My friend Gene from Columbia South Carolina has printed on the mirrors on his pickup truck "OBJECTS IN MIRROR ARE LOOSING." When I commented about it Gene told me that "it doesn't do any good to look in the rearview mirror anyway, if you know where you are going, your goal is ahead of you."

How do you keep your eyes on the road ahead?

- Celebrate – then move on.
- Erect a monument to your success if you need to – but move on.
- Acknowledge mistakes – then move on.
- Take responsibility – then move on.
- Get up early – and move on.
- Read to learn, soak up knowledge - and move on.
- Seek advice and set new goals, act on them – and move on.
- Self-sooth – BE happy – BE focused – BE calmly alert – and move on.
- Know where you are going – and move on.
- Don't let memories be greater than your dreams – and move on.
- Move on.

From:	SabelTheCat
Sent:	11:01 PM
To:	Tim
Subject:	Mind Your Own Beeswax

Attn. Large Hairless Subordinate:

It's my ping pong ball, and I am NOT playing with it wrong if I bat it around on the tile floors at night. So take it out of the cupboard, put it back on the floor, and mind your own business!

STC

Do you like to be seen as a high-achieving, aligned, focused, progressive leader and influencer? If the answer is "yes, of course, I do!" then you depend on inculcating peer feedback into your real-time personal development plan.

What kind of feedback should take action on?
> Constructive
> Consistent
> Timely
> Tangible
> Concrete, specific, and useful
> Transparent, user-friendly and not overwhelming
> Practical and fits the setting it is offered in

Non-judgmental

Any feedback that demonstrates these characteristics will help you focus on creating real leadership value.

Ken Blanchard wisely noted that "feedback is the breakfast of champions."

From:	SabelTheCat
Sent:	8:00 AM
To:	Tim
Subject:	Control Freakery

Attn. Large Hairless Subordinate:

It has come to my attention that you are a control freak. That you believe "it is all about you." You make the rules – Don't wake you up at the crack of 2 AM, don't sing you the sweet lullaby of the caterwaul peoples when you want to nap, don't put artistic claw marks on the new sofa so it doesn't look so 'store-bought.' It's something for you to work on.

STC

Do you fear disorganization? Does chaos send you into a fugue? Do you love the spotlight and getting all the credit and attention? Do you trust yourself more than others to get stuff done, on time, and correctly? High standards that no one else seems to be able to uphold? High levels of anxiety when not the leader? Are you an egotistical show-off?

You are a control freak. Stop that! Just take control – take control-freakery by the horns, and stop it! You are severely destructive in respect to your crucial relationships and ultimately doing yourself a great deal of psychological and even physical harm.

Start small if you have to, let your spouse decide the brand of coffee to buy, and work your way up to letting your better half choose the make and model of the family car. Finally, give yourself and all of us a break and acknowledge that you simply cannot control everything. Delegate some of the important work to your competent team, and let them shine. That ego needs the boot as well. It's non-negotiable, it has to happen. We all recognize your poisonous behavior, it is keeping you from being a success and taints our best efforts as your colleagues as well.

This is an intervention.

From:	SabelTheCat
Sent:	1:32 AM
To:	Tim
Subject:	Revenge

Attn. Large Hairless Subordinate:

Remember tonight when you put me through the humiliation of trimming the tips of my claws? They will grow back and that new living room upholstery needs a good 'breaking in.'

STC

There is nothing that sends the signal that a person lacks the emotional competency required for leadership more than seeing someone in a position of influence that openly and deliberately seeks revenge. Revenge is a tell-tale indicator of a tendency to make poor management decisions. Why? Because revenge is a violation of a rudimentary, and foundational business principle... The principle of 'sunk cost.' Business economic theory proposes that a cogent actor does not let sunk costs influence a decision because the past cannot be recovered. They distinguish sunk costs as the costs that have already been incurred, and as such; it not rational to expect that they can be recovered to any substantial degree moving forward. In terms of emotional competency, this is mirrored in the 'fallacy of bygones principle.'

Instead of wasting momentum on revenge (which is a sunk cost expressed in 'bygones') leaders listen more deeply, speak only briefly, and pay attention to non-verbal cues early in an engagement so the sunk cost of injury is more likely to never be expensed. Once the infraction is made, however; the emotionally competent leader will forgive the cost of the bygone, and set out on a new course with new decisions since the past cannot be changed and we have only the present and the future ahead of us.

This is more than just turning the other cheek; it is more than personal humility. We look to leaders to be people who are competent even to the point of putting their emotions in check so they can effectively lead us into the future.

From:	SabelTheCat
Sent:	11:00 AM
To:	Tim
Subject:	Now – Now – NOW!

Attn. Large Hairless Subordinate:

Scratch my belly... NOW! Stop... NOW! BITE BITE BITE!

STC

"If you want to conquer the anxiety of life, live in the moment, live in the breath." — Amit Ray, Om Chanting and Meditation

Ever wonder where your energy went? It is likely more of a question of "when" you can find it, rather than 'where.' The present, the 'now', is the only reality that we can choose to affect. It is a tangible point in time between any measurement of the past and the future. The present is always there and is the only moment in time that we can access for any purpose. Everything that transpires, everything that you do, can only occur in the present moment. It is impossible to bring anything into existence outside of it.

The past and the present don't possess discrete reality. They are simply conceptual descriptions of present experiences past, or an idea of what is to come, by happenstance, plan, or causality.

- Let go of the past.
- Believe the course you laid in for the future.
- Breathe.
- Exist in the moment.
- Know where you are going.
- Find your energy.

From:	SabelTheCat
Sent:	3:00 PM
To:	Tim
Subject:	Interrupting Nap Time

Attn. Large Hairless Subordinate:

If you learn nothing else, it should be not to interrupt my nap time. If you doubt me, consult the hairball I left in your bedroom slipper.

STC

Continuous reading...

Self-improvement

Business

Lectures

Travel

History

White papers

The Art of War – by Sun Tzu

The Prince - by Niccolo Machiavelli

Obvious Adams - by Robert R. Updegraff

It Works - by Anonymous

Jab, Jab, Jab, Right Hook - By Gary Vaynerchuk

Perfecting Your Pitch – by Ronald M. Shapiro
The Song of Solomon, The Acts of the Apostles, The Gospel of Thomas

... Continuous improvement.

From:	SabelTheCat
Sent:	10:15 PM
To:	Tim
Subject:	Think about ME for once in a row

Attn. Large Hairless Subordinate:

It's very unattractive when you are so self-centered. You didn't notice that you stopped scratching my chin after only 7 minutes but I did! It's something to work on.

STC

Many people in positions of influence build tremendous strategic organizations, leaders engage employees and customers with purpose. Strategy tells Michael Jordan to dribble, run, and jump... Purpose tells him to put the brown thing in the round thing! A basketball court with no hoops to shoot at is a strategic enterprise without purpose.

Purpose is your sense of 'being'... You find yourself leading with purpose because you are contributing to something of great importance. The mission is what purpose-driven leaders like you square themselves with. A great strategy comes from what you know and draws from your experience... Strategy comes from your sense of self. You value purpose and mission above 'self' and short-term accomplishment. You look to the long-term gains; you turn shirtsleeves inside-out; you find no comfort in the status quo, you have no inclination to settle or for the shallowness of success just to take credit. It's not about you, it likely never was.

From:	SabelTheCat
Sent:	4: 25 AM
To:	Tim
Subject:	My Excuse, Please Acknowledge

Attn. Large Hairless Subordinate:

Do or do not buy better kibble, there is no try*. But, I would appreciate it if you would 'try' to find the crunchy salmon flavor kind.

STC

* adapted from Yoda - Star Wars: Episode V - The Empire Strikes Back (1980)

Having trouble getting started? Can't find a way – or – find an excuse? Let me help!

- Maybe you don't have time.
- I'll bet someone else will probably just ruin it if you do it.
- It is clearly someone else's turn.
- You really don't want to fail.
- You will probably just gain the weight back – backslide – get distracted – drop out.
- I think you are too tired.
- It is definitely beyond your skill set – above your paygrade – out of your reach.

- Fast food is easier.
- 9-5 is all that is required and compensated for.
- You don't want to be called a brown nose – a b!#ch – teacher's pet.
- You don't know how to start a business – write a book – play guitar.
- This is nuts – crazy - an insane endeavor - a fool's folly.

It hurts when I say destructive things about you getting started on accomplishing the fruits of your own boundless potential doesn't it? Well, it hurts your family, your friends, your colleagues, and the "future you" when you do it too. Stop that. You got this… Find a way and throw the excuses out.

From:	SabelTheCat
Sent:	7:53 PM
To:	Tim
Subject:	Stick a fork in me...

Attn. Large Hairless Subordinate:

... I'm done! Enough is enough... I'll be napping and I hope you have this mess cleaned up and have made my life better by the time I get up.

STC

While no one is likely to clean up your mess for you, Sabel has a good idea in that she is seeking out a silver lining. When you are exhausted, you will be in a good state of mind for quiet reflection, rest, and recuperation... Then you can approach the silver lining of focused energy when you emerge from your meditation or your power-nap.

Other common silver linings?

Did you just learn that you have a reputation of being impulsive? The positive side of that coin is that you are spontaneous. The silver lining being that you are likely the person who always knows a good place to catch a bite to eat, a great movie you have been wanting to see, a suggestion for a book to read, an initiative to launch, the path to take for a great walk.

Lose your job? Time to connect with your network of colleagues. Find a career in a new field or a familiar one with renewed sense of vigor.

Disorganized, cluttered, messy? You are in a creative time of your life. Get in the creative flow!

You were called intimidating. You are probably naturally assertive. Focus it on standing up for a good cause, fighting the good fight, bearing someone's burden who can't fight for themselves.

Whatever the concern is that is making you peer into the abyss, to try to find the hope beyond hope, just know that we all walk the same path to discover the silver lining and the steps along the journey are the same...

- ✓ Journal
- ✓ Get out
- ✓ Sketch – paint – draw – photograph something
- ✓ Experiment
- ✓ Be social
- ✓ Follow up with old friends – make a new one
- ✓ Read a book – read a few books
- ✓ Learn a new skill (A friend once asked me if I knew how to play Blueberry Hill on the piano... I said that I didn't, so he told me I at least know a skill to pick up when I am at a loss for something new to learn... I know – it's kinda weird, but I keep it in mind, so it works for me.)
- ✓ Use sticky notes – put them all over – mind map
- ✓ Break the routine
- ✓ Spend time in the company of creative people
- ✓ Spy – on the competition
- ✓ Go to a gallery – showing – art installation
- ✓ Collaborate
- ✓ Travel
- ✓ A new hobby

- ✓ A new challenge
- ✓ Make a new list
- ✓ Ask for feedback
- ✓ Listen deeply to music – poetry – the ocean – the rain – steak frying – a cat purring
- ✓ Watch a great movie
- ✓ Take that risk
- ✓ Declutter
- ✓ Clutter up a pile to enjoy the free-association
- ✓ Love
- ✓ Finish
- ✓ Be affectionate
- ✓ Journal your dreams
- ✓ Take a nap
- ✓ Practice
- ✓ Eat something new
- ✓ Question the status quo
- ✓ Shut off distractions
- ✓ Let go of fear
- ✓ Be curious
- ✓ And for heaven's sake, stop comparing yourself to others!

CHAPTER 17 - GOSSIP

From:	SabelTheCat
Sent:	2:38 PM
To:	Tim
Subject:	Did you hear what she said?

Attn. Large Hairless Subordinate:

Your mate said she wants a dog. A DOG! I have noticed she is drinking the caramel-colored, crazy-making, cactus juice a lot more since last Cinco De Mayo ... I think you need to do an intervention before she gets you to give in and let her get a nasty dog.

STC

At our best as leaders we hit our stride when talking about innovative ideas, certainly not gossiping about other people. Trust and gossip simply can't coexist, but if your organization is trudging through times of low trust, gossip and rumors spark up almost spontaneously and begin to wick resources and imagination away from meaningful work and accomplishment.

- Intercede.
- Confront gossip head-on.
- Coach offenders.

- Double-up the crystal-clear communication in times of uncertainty and organizational ambiguity.
- Use multiple, diverse channels to communicate the truth.
- Support open dialog.
- Archetype a no-gossip policy.
- Lead by example.

From:	SabelTheCat
Sent:	5:42 AM
To:	Tim
Subject:	Nope...

Attn. Large Hairless Subordinate:

Didn't see who clawed the curtains. No idea. Stop being so accusatory, it is not a very attractive trait. It's something to work on.

STC

The value of ethical behavior can be found in...

> ... modeling ethical behavior to the organization and the community.
> ... building trust.
> ... allowing personal and organizational credibility and respect to develop.
> ... making the workplace more conducive to collaboration.
> ... developing a sense of team security.
> ... occupying the moral high ground.
> ... doing the right thing.
> ... generating self-respect.

From: SabelTheCat
Sent: 3:47 AM
To: Tim
Subject: My Share

Attn. Large Hairless Subordinate:

It has come to my attention that you have taken to sitting sideways with your legs elevated, leaving precious little room for me to lie comfortably on my half of the over-stuffed scratching post you call 'the couch.' Please sit straight so I can take my share... Out of the middle.

STC

There is a distinct value to a leader's demonstrations of heartfelt gratefulness that the "entitled authoritarians" in an organization never realize. For instance: An appreciated associate is a motivated associate; when employees hear about how their work is making a difference for the better they will strive for consistent results; morale is intensified simply by acknowledging your team by thanking them for doing great work; when your team feels valued they are less likely to wander, looking for greener pastures.

Build a delta of gratefulness between the "entitled" yourself by thanking the team, thanking an individual, being genuine, specific, and spontaneous. You can even be downright unexpected, so the team never knows when lighting will strike and one of them will be singled out as a stellar performer. It's exciting and motivating to contribute to a team where recognition means that the stars that shine in the firmament of the division, company, or trade are pointed out as examples of extraordinary accomplishment.

Leadership is for those who are grateful to be influencing a team to accomplish amazing things together and can show that gratitude effectively. Leadership is not the product of an entitlement program.

From:	SabelTheCat
Sent:	5:12 PM
To:	Tim
Subject:	Meowie is meeeeeee

Attn. Large Hairless Subordinate:

As I have mentioned before... The kibble is mine... Mama's lap = mine... The good spot on the couch = mine, the middle step on the staircase where I like to sleep at night = mine. These are all mine, please stop rationing kibble and chasing me out of my favorite places. It's something for you to work on.

STC

Sabel's version of ownership is entertaining but misses the mark of an effective leader that takes productive ownership over all the things they have influence over. I have known great leaders that take ownership seriously, they always find a way, they can do, they choose to do, and they will do. I have also known people in positions of influence and authority to approach their responsibilities as if they are victims... They know they will fail, there are things they should do, can't do, have to do, but they will quit long before they get a good start.

- Leaders show ownership by finding a way when victims find excuses.
- It's focusing on improvement instead of fearing your weakness.
- Accepting responsibility instead of placing blame.
- Treating problems as temporary setbacks instead of permanent conditions.
- Asking for a new perspective rather than complaining about the circumstance.
- Seek help from smarter, more experienced, or more highly skilled individuals rather than feeling inadequate and hiding those short-comings from the organization with a management smokescreen and subterfuge.
- Do something creative rather than repeat ineffective but familiar processes.
- Look for a better, next choice rather than just give up.
- Do versus try.

Blessings!

Timothy Hagler is an experienced life sciences supply chain leader, with an ever-accelerating interest in earnestly connecting stakeholders with creative ideas to meet new economic realities for healthcare providers. Tim has enjoyed an excellent track record of achievement and advancement earned through demonstrated contribution to bottom-line results, employing strong solutions architecture, analytic and financial skills in challenging, multi-client environments. Tim and his lovely wife Kandy enjoy spending time at the beach in South Carolina. Tim's hobbies include photography, American folk music, and writing about himself in the third person.

Contact the author at: tim@thinkoutsideinsupplychain.com

Visit the author's healthcare supply chain and leadership blog at:

http://www.thinkoutsideinsupplychain.com/

www.ingramcontent.com/pod-product-compliance
Lightning Source LLC
Chambersburg PA
CBHW070407190526
45169CB00003B/1150